Robert Allen **Palmer**, born on 19th January 1949, Batley, West Yorkshire, E
songwriter, musician & record producer, best known for his powerful, dist
and sartorial elegance, combined soul, jazz, rock, pop, reggae & blues. Rok
music industry began during the '60s, spanning 4 decades, including a period with the group Vinegar
Joe. He was successful both in his solo career and with the Power Station, having had Top 10 songs in
both the UK & the US in the '80s.

Three of his hit singles, 'I Didn't Mean to Turn You On', 'Addicted to Love' and 'Simply Irresistible',
were supported by stylish music videos directed by British fashion photographer Terence Donovan.
Palmer won several awards during his career, including a couple of Grammy Awards for Best Male
Rock Vocal Performance & an MTV Video Music Award, having also received 2 Brit Award
nominations for Best British Male Solo Artist. He passed away at the age of 54, after having a heart
attack on 26th September 2003.

Robert's dad was a British naval intelligence officer stationed in Malta, who took his family from
Batley to Scarborough during 1949, when Robert was just 3 months old. Influenced by blues, soul and
jazz music on American Forces Radio, while a youth, Palmer joined his 1st band, The Mandrakes,
when aged 15, whilst a pupil of Scarborough High School for Boys. His 1st big break came with the
departure of singer Jess Roden from the group The Alan Bown Set in 1969, following which Robert
was invited to London to sing on their single 'Gypsy Girl'. The vocals for their eponymous L.P. The Alan
Bown Set!, originally recorded by Roden, as issued in the States, were re-recorded by Palmer after the
single became a hit. Music journalist Paul Lester stated that Robert left behind northern clubs in
England to become an 'elegant and sophisticated' master of several styles.

He joined the 12-piece jazz-rock fusion band Dada during 1970, featuring singer Elkie Brooks & her
husband Pete Gage. Palmer, Brooks and Gage formed soul/rock group Vinegar Joe a year later, in
which Robert played rhythm guitar, while sharing lead vocals with Elkie. After signing with the Island
Records label, they issued 3 albums: Vinegar Joe (1972), Rock 'n' Roll Gypsies (1972) then Six Star
General (1973), before breaking up in March 1974. Brooks later said that Palmer "was a very good-
looking guy", so female fans were happy that the pair weren't romantically linked.

Island Records signed Robert to a solo deal during 1974, his 1st solo L.P. Sneakin' Sally Through the
Alley, recorded in New Orleans, Louisiana that year being heavily influenced by the music of Little
Feat & the funk fusion of the Meters, who acted as backing band, along with producer/guitarist Lowell
George of Little Feat. Although a failure in the UK, both the album and single made the Top 100 in the
US. 'Sailin' Shoes', the L.P's first track, a Little Feat cover, along with Palmer's own 'Hey Julia' & the
Allen Toussaint-penned title track had virtually the same rhythm, being packaged on the album as a
'trilogy' without a pause between them.

After moving to New York City with his wife, Robert released Pressure Drop, named after the cover
version of the reggae hit by Toots and the Maytals, in November 1975, featuring Motown bassist
James Jamerson. Palmer toured with Little Feat to promote the reggae & rock-infused L.P. then
following the failure of follow-up album Some People Can Do What They Like he decided to relocate
to Nassau, Bahamas, just across the street from Compass Point Studios.

Robert issued Double Fun (1978), a collection of Caribbean-influenced rock, including a cover of 'You
Really Got Me'. The L.P. entered the Top 50 of the US Billboard chart, producing a hit single with the
Andy Fraser-penned 'Every Kinda People' (US # 16), which has been covered by other artists including
Chaka Demus and Pliers, Randy Crawford, The Mint Juleps, produced by Trevor Horn, & Amy Grant.
Palmer's next album focused on pure rock, 'Secrets' (1979) producing his 2nd Top 20 single with
Moon Martin's 'Bad Case of Loving You (Doctor, Doctor)' hitting US #14, his 2nd Billboard Hot 100
year-end chart hit.

Robert became increasingly successful during the '80s, the L.P. Clues, which he produced, featuring
Chris Frantz & Gary Numan, gave hits on both sides of the Atlantic, 1st with the radio-friendly single
'Johnny and Mary' then 'Looking for Clues'. Catchy music videos with the synth-pop stylings of new

wave increased Palmer's exposure to a younger audience, leading to another hit with the EP release of Some Guys Have All the Luck in 1982.

'Pride' was issued during April of the following year, which, although not as big a hit as 'Looking for Clues', featured the title song and Robert's cover of The System's 'You Are in My System', with the group's David Frank contributing keyboard tracks to the latter song. Palmer's concert at the Hammersmith Palais on 31st May 1983 was recorded then broadcast on BBC Radio 1. He performed at Duran Duran's charity concert at Aston Villa football ground on 23rd July of that year, where he made friends with members of the band that led to the formation of super-group the Power Station.

When Duran Duran had a break, guitarist Andy Taylor & bassist John Taylor joined Robert and former Chic drummer Tony Thompson to form the Power Station. Their self-titled album, recorded mainly at the New York recording studio after which the band was named, with overdubs & mixing at Compass Point Studios in Nassau, Bahamas, made the UK Top 20 then the US Top 10. It produced a couple of hit singles; 'Some Like It Hot' (US # 6) plus a cover of the T. Rex tune 'Get It On (Bang a Gong)', which went one higher than the original (US # 9).

Palmer performed live with the super-group only once that year, on Saturday Night Live. The band toured, playing Live Aid with singer Michael Des Barres after Robert pulled out at the last minute to go back into the recording studio to develop his solo career, which some critics described as unprofessional. In Number One magazine he refuted the suggestion that he'd joined the group out of greed: "Firstly, I didn't need the money, 2ndly the cash was a long time coming. It wasn't exactly an experience that set me up for retirement". Palmer, who was also accused of ripping off the Power Station sound on his own records, responded: "Listen, I gave the Power Station that sound. They took it from me, not the other way around".

He recorded the L.P. Riptide at Compass Point Studios during 1985, recruiting Thompson and Andy Taylor to play on some tracks, along with Power Station record producer Bernard Edwards, who worked with Thompson in Chic, to head the production. Riptide featured the US chart-topping single 'Addicted to Love', which hit UK # 5, supported by a memorable, much-imitated music video, directed by Terence Donovan, in which Robert was surrounded by near-identically clad, heavily made-up female models simulating 'musicians'. Terence also directed videos for his hits 'Simply Irresistible' & 'I Didn't Mean to Turn You On'.

Palmer performed 'Addicted to Love' at the MTV Video Music Awards in Los Angeles in September 1986 then won the Grammy Award for Best Male Rock Vocal Performance for it the following year. He received his 1st nomination for Best British Male at the Brit Awards of 1987. His cover of Cherrelle's 'I Didn't Mean to Turn You On', also sold well, hitting US # 2 and UK # 9, while another song, 'Trick Bag', was written by one of his major influences, New Orleans jazz musician Earl King. Alarmed by the rising crime rate in Nassau, Robert moved to Lugano, Switzerland during 1987, setting up his own recording studio. Producing Heavy Nova the following year, he began experimenting again, with bossa nova rhythms, heavy rock & white-soul balladeering.

Palmer repeated his success of 'Addicted to Love' with the video of 'Simply Irresistible', again with a troupe of female 'musicians', which hit US # 2, his last Top Ten hit in the States. The ballad 'She Makes My Day' also became a hit in Britain, making UK # 6. He won a 2nd Grammy in 1989, for 'Simply Irresistible', which was later featured in the Tony Award-winning musical 'Contact'. Robert was nominated for Best British Male for the 2nd time at that year's Brit Awards, where 'Simply Irresistible' was nominated for Best British Single.

Rolling Stone magazine named him the best-dressed rock star of 1990, Palmer further expanding his range that year for his next album 'Don't Explain', which produced a couple of UK top 10 hits; covers of Bob Dylan's 'I'll Be Your Baby Tonight', a collaboration with UB40, and Marvin Gaye's 'Mercy Mercy Me'. He ventured further into diverse material during the '90s, with his L.P. 'Ridin' High' (1992), being a tribute to the Tin Pan Alley era.

Robert released 'Honey' in 1994, which received mixed reviews, the album failing to produce any US hit singles, although in the UK he issued 3 modest hit singles 'Girl U Want', 'Know by Now' then 'You Blow Me Away'. Palmer released a greatest hits L.P. the following year, which hit UK # 4, reuniting with other members of Power Station during 1995 to record a 2nd album, although bassist John Taylor pulled out of the project, being replaced by Bernard Edwards. Robert & the rest of the band completed the L.P. Living in Fear (1996), having just begun touring when Edwards died from pneumonia. Palmer performed with Rod Stewart at Wembley the following year.

Robert met Sue, a fabric designer, his future wife, at Slough railway station in 1969, attracted by her style, clad in silver-coloured boots with a matching mini-dress, plus the science-fiction book that she was reading. The couple wed 2 years later then had a couple of kids. The family moved to New York City during the mid-'70s then to the Bahamas a few years later, followed by Lugano, Switzerland in 1987, before divorcing during 1999. A quiet man in his private life, Palmer wasn't interested in excesses of the rock 'n' roll lifestyle but he was a heavy smoker, getting through up to 60 cigarettes / day.

Robert had a sudden massive heart attack when in a Paris hotel room on 26th September 2003, passing away at the age of 54, having travelled there after recording the retrospective 'My Kinda People' in London for Yorkshire TV. His long-term partner, Mary Ambrose, wasn't with Palmer when he died. Duran Duran paid tribute stating: "He was a very dear friend and a great artist. This is a tragic loss to the British music industry". He was buried in Lugano, Switzerland.

Discography

Studio albums

Sneakin' Sally Through the Alley (1974)
Pressure Drop (1975)
Some People Can Do What They Like (1976)
Double Fun (1978)
Secrets (1979)
Clues (1980)
Maybe It's Live (1982) (Half studio tracks, half live)
Pride (1983)
Riptide (1985)
Heavy Nova (1988)
Don't Explain (1990)
Ridin' High (1992)
Honey (1994)
Rhythm & Blues (1999)
Drive (2003)

Could it have been a coincidence that Hedi Slimane, one of the fashion industry's biggest rock'n'roll fan-boys, chose the '80s as the inspiration for his final collection of Saint Laurent during 2016, the 30th anniversary of that most '80s of rock videos, Robert Palmer's Addicted to Love? The collection had all the hallmarks of the girls that graced his video - LBDs, sheer, 10 denier tights and with a blusher and red lipstick quota that must've made backstage make-up artists busier than usual.

Along with moody expressions, cinched-in belts & the kind of pointy stilettos that only the '80s could produce, there was little doubt that Addicted to Love was on heavy rotation in Slimane's L.A. studio. Other designers weren't immune to its charms, Slimane's rumoured successor, Anthony Vaccarello, Versace and Vetements having had a touch of the Palmers over the past few seasons, while American Apparel had been selling the look on the high street for ages.

There were few pop videos that still managed to feel relevant after 30 years, especially one that really only involved a backdrop of photo-wall paper with a 'band' of girls in black dresses, fronted by Robert in a kind of estate-agent-after-work look of black trousers, white shirt and black tie. With over 24 million views on YouTube, it had been parodied by Weird Al Yankovich, having inspired the opposite treatment from Shania Twain in her video for 'Man! I Feel Like a Woman,' in which she fronted a group flanked by male models on guitars. The women-as-glambots thing felt a bit dated, but not in comparison to Blurred Lines. The girls-with-guitars, man in a suit thing had become commonplace, the girls were just wearing a lot less.

Regarding fashion, it was the full package, clothes included, that made Addicted to Love so irresistible. The look was apparently based on the artwork of Patrick Nagel, who drew the girl on the cover of Duran Duran's Rio, hence the mask-like faces. Model Julia Bolino, the guitarist on the far right, said in 2013 that the toughest thing about the video was "having lipgloss applied every 3 seconds". The route 1 idea of fierce sexiness; red lips, slicked-back hair & tight black Alaia-like dresses, was still effective, and after years of 'no makeup-makeup', boho floaty layers & sportswear, it was subversively, almost excessively, glamorous. In a world where day-to-night dressing had become the norm, with contouring meaning a makeup bag full of beige shades, proper transforming makeup like that, worn with a cocktail dress, was categorically after-dark, feeling edgy.

Part of the video's longevity came from its pedigree, being directed by Terence Donovan, the photographer who had captured the '60s in London for Vogue and Man About Town a couple of decades earlier. He was part of the MTV-fuelled video explosion, directing it along with Palmer's promo for Simply Irresistible, having also worked for Toyah, Malcolm McLaren and Liza Minelli. All had the kind of lighting, composition & drama - with Minelli in an off-the-shoulder gown and girls in formation in a steam room for McLaren's Madame Butterfly - that you'd expect from a Vogue photographer. After adding styling by Harper's Bazaar editor Liz Tilberis then Addicted to Love became a moving, high-end fashion shoot. Whereas most other mid-'80s shoots had been consigned to fashion history, this bit of pop culture history had remained on the mood-board, as 3 decades on, we were still addicted to Addicted to Love.

The British star Robert Palmer best known for his hits 'Addicted to Love', 'Some Guys Have All the Luck' and 'Didn't Mean to Turn You On' had died of a heart attack in Paris aged 54. He'd been in the city on a 2-day break with partner Mary Ambrose, following recording a TV appearance in the London. His manager said that he'd suffered the heart attack during the early hours of Friday 26th September 2003. The Batley-born singer had recently been on a tour of Europe to promote his latest L.P. 'Drive'.

Robert had been performing since 1969, playing in groups including Mandrake Paddle Steamer & Dada, featuring Elkie Brooks, going on to front Vinegar Joe with Brooks, issuing 3 albums with the band before launching his solo career. Elkie said that she was "devastated" at the news, having reconciled with Palmer after several "differences of opinion" over the years. "Robert was a star - he was a great writer, a fabulous musician, a great singer & he was stunning looking". She said that he had a big influence over other artists, especially visually, with his ground-breaking videos. "Robert was always one that wanted to be different, wanted to be trendy - from the way he looked to the music. He wanted to be a step ahead," Brooks added.

He was also a member of '80s supergroup Power Station, which included members of Duran Duran. It was during that decade that Palmer got mainstream solo recognition. Suzanne Parkes, who worked as his publicist for Power Station's Living in Fear album (1996), stated: "He was something really rare in the music industry, his offstage persona was even nicer than that on-stage he was an absolute gent. I'm really sad, I remember the times with Robert as just so much fun. I recall going with him to this secret karaoke club in Soho once , when he got up on stage to sing karaoke to his own songs, to Addicted to Love, just for a laugh". One of rock music's most famous videos 'Addicted to Love', featured Robert backed by a 'band' of identically-dressed women, who were made up to look the same.

After having hits with She Makes My Day and Mercy Mercy Me he turned he returned to his rhythm 'n' blues roots, with his Ridin' High L.P. of 1992 being a mix of genres from Tin Pan Alley and cabaret classics. Palmer's greatest hits album was put out during 1995, reaching UK # 4. Born in Batley, West Yorkshire, he spent much of his childhood in Malta before moving back to the UK at the age of 19, where his family settled in Scarborough. Later he spent lived in New York, the Bahamas & Switzerland, but stayed close to his roots.

Rock journalist Paul Lester said of Robert: "He was kind of a pioneer of blue-eyed soul, which is white men doing black music and R&B pretty well. He had 2 or 3 careers". Palmer had shot his parts for a regional TV show, My Kinda People, about his musical influences, for Yorkshire TV on the Wednesday before he died, having appeared on stage with Chaka Khan at Wembley Arena not long before: "At the moment, no decision has been made regarding the future of this programme as everyone's thoughts are with Robert's family and friends," a spokesman said.

Vinegar Joe appeared at Reading Festival 3 months after they issued their 1st L.P. with Island Records. In the 3 years that the band existed, from 1971 - 1974, they released 3 albums. They were never huge, but were very popular with students, playing a lot on the university circuit. Appearing at a festival was always a real high point for the group, Brooks recalling the time"Vividly, Status Quo, whom we used to support quite often, were also in the line-up.

Robert Palmer and I were very competitive; I suppose that was understandable because we were both lead singers in Vinegar Joe, but outside the group we used to get on very well. When we were on the road we'd often go off on our own, find a bistro then enjoy a nice bottle of wine & a meal together, although mostly we lived on food from motorway services, because we weren't paid much. Robert was a very good-looking guy, so girls that we met used to be well pleased when they found out that we weren't an item. I used to buy a lot of my outfits for the stage from second-hand shops and the antique market on the King's Road in London.

I lived around the corner in Fulham. I remember this bikini-type top very well. I embroidered my name on it with diamanté, just in case you didn't know who I was & a fan gave me the skirt, which came with a matching top. I really found myself when I was in Vinegar Joe, becoming very outgoing and uninhibited. I'd issued my 1st record, 'Something's Got A Hold On Me', in 1964. It didn't do very well and, despite touring with the Animals then supporting the Beatles for 3 weeks, I lacked confidence. After Vinegar Joe, during 1977, when I'd given up thinking I was ever going to get anything in the pop charts, my single Pearl's A Singer hit # 8. It was released on my birthday, February 25th.

I think Island Records always saw Vinegar Joe as something of a rehearsal band for Robert. When we split up the whole group was definitely smarting for a few months. Robert felt that I was very pissed off & although I really never held a grudge we didn't keep in touch, our paths never crossed, which was a huge shame. I kept in touch with his parents and his brother, who've been to my shows over the years. I admired Robert so much and I recorded his song 'Circles' for my L.P. of the same name in 1995. If that isn't a tribute to his great ability, then what is?".

Robert Palmer quite possibly thought that he was 'it' but that was OK, because in a way, he was right. A native Batley boy, he'd made judicious use of his fine voice - a baritone, he could also sing tenor or falsetto, a whopping range - eclectic musical tastes, including Detroit rhythm, reggae, bossa nova, techno-kraut, along with a debonair demeanour, to establish an almost unassailable place in the rock canon.

Some contended that Palmer was cheated of the status he deserved - the average Joe probably only knowing him for mid-'80s stomps, especially 'Addicted to Love', memories being of the notorious video of long-legged, possibly lobotomised, guitar-wielding lovelies. However, he had the respect of his peers, a sumptuous lifestyle, a home on the Swiss-Italian border, with his latest album recorded in Capri, which would all tend to make one well pleased with oneself.

Aged 50, despite stating that "Good living has blurred my once-taut outline", Robert was in powerful form, as he'd demonstrated at a showcase that February, when in a room of Thai-food-chomping sales managers, he delivered maximum Bob. Backed by a gospel choir, he mixed new tracks with gems from the past but, unsurprisingly, it was the raunchy, sex-beast stuff that went down best - rock from a time before Loaded or FHM but somehow prefiguring them: GQ with its tie loosened and its shirt undone. Palmer, in trademark suit, sweated the show like the soul man he was, rending his hair while grimacing, his hand movements ornate & geisha-like, with his well-shod feet so tiny that they might once have been bound.

A few days later Robert was sitting at the table in his hotel room smoking, being half-way through a pitcher of Bloody Mary at 10.30am, having waved away tea or coffee with a curl of the lip. He seemed to have the constitution of a tank, with a cragginess to his playboy looks. In an Armani 2-piece and wire-rimmed glasses, he had the air of a slightly malevolent, louchely stylish, doctor: "I'm intolerant of incompetents & ignorance. That's one thing I recognise about my age; I used to suffer fools, but I won't now", he stated. It was this that made some judge him as arrogant, although his self-assurance had been his lodestar. Having studied comparative religion, he believed in a composite god. Where did he look for reassurance? "To my inner harmony." He pointed to his chest, laughing, as if it were obvious. "That's where God is".

Though born in Yorkshire, at just 3 months old Palmer's family moved to Malta, where his father worked in naval intelligence. A solitary boy, he'd accompany his parents to the glamorous balls of the international expatriate community. There, on American Forces radio, he heard Lena Horne, Sinatra and Nat King Cole, while soaking up a soigne approach to life. He became obsessed with the uniforms of the Italian naval officers - "They looked happening", growing fanatical over the neatness of his school wear.

It wasn't vanity insisted: "I've always been fastidious about clothes. It's a psychological thing, I suppose. I don't like to get dirty". The globe-trotting artist had an accent that blended Batley with Los Angeles - Michael Parkinson goes Valley Girl, or maybe Alan Bennett. He said of a recent tour of the States, where he was again depressed by messiness: "St Louis was - Whoah! It'd gone downhill, it was scruffy..." Years later, when he began performing, the immaculate Marvin Gaye & Otis Redding were his arbiters of taste. A suit was a disguise, as he said that he was painfully shy. "It's what you do, not how it looks. Thank God I never got tied up in any silly fashions - I nearly mentioned Bryan Ferry, but he had a feather boa, didn't he? - he had to look back, dying of embarrassment".

The family returned to England, the poor weather coming as a nasty shock, where aged 12 Robert began guitar lessons with "A little old lady who burned a paraffin stove. 1st tune was `The Girl from Ipanema'". After leaving school he had a stint at art college, where the curriculum "didn't encourage artistry", so he left to develop his R&B tastes. Aged 19 he got his 1st professional singing job then met his wife to be, Sue, a fabric designer, at Slough station: "I was taken by her style. Silver boots and silver mini-dress. The '60s, y'know?" Did he just introduce himself? "Well, she was also reading a science fiction book, I'm a sci-fi fan".

Palmer was a private man but, despite the humping, grinding mid-period hits, in which the quest for random sex was brainlessly urgent, his personal life had been famously settled, although the couple had got divorced over 10 years earlier. Back in 1973, he was spotted singing with Elkie Brooks in Vinegar Joe by Island records' MD Chris Blackwell, who flew him to New Orleans to set him up to record his debut album with legendary funk stalwarts, The Meters:

"To begin with, there was a definite impression of, `What's the white boy doin' here?' 10 minutes into the session, we hit a real big pocket & it got hot. The drummer stood up then said: `Hey, what's your name?' From then on, we rocked". They made 'Sneakin' Sally through the Alley', which was a cult hit but despite sophisticated follow-ups, the gorgeous singles from them - 'Every Kinda People', 'Johnny and Mary', 'Looking for Clues', 'Some Guys Have All the Luck' - only sold fairly well.

Joining the lumbering Power Station, with Duran Duran's John and Andy Taylor brought Robert worldwide stardom during 1984; the L.P. that he made when he left, 'Riptide', was his 1st chart-topper, featuring 'Addicted to Love', with its incendiary video . 2 years later, Heavy Nova continued the video formula, with 'Simply Irresistible' & 'I Didn't Mean to Turn You On' that offended some but went platinum.

Later albums came and went unnoticed, which almost didn't matter, as he'd been able to bring up his kids in the Bahamas then move to the chocolate-box town of Lugano but Palmer had his pride. His 1st album for 5 years 'Rhythm & Blues', mixed romance with solid grooving, one or two eccentricities, a lost jewel from Little Feat's Lowell George and a cover of Marvin Gaye's 'Let's Get it On'. Was he pleased with it?

"Some of it's blatantly erotic. Just being honest. First thing anyone notices about somebody is what sex they are". When not working, Robert liked to read, or irritate his teenage son & daughter by cranking up Motorhead or Rannstein. - "German goth band... Wooh, they're fantastic!". He kept his cigarette case full, except when he was performing, remaining a bon viveur "Then it's another belt-hole. For whom the belt holes...". He always stated that he never took drugs, although he'd say "Ah - I just never admitted it", but Palmer didn't need them, anyway. "I didn't used to be able to sit down... I thought that unless I was running around I'd vanish. Now I'm real good at relaxing. Light a fire, put the slippers on, watch TV." He looked up. Even talking about slippers, he was suave. "It's such a buzz doing that".

The famous video, featuring a clutch of gloss-lipped, black mini-skirted, deadpan models posing as backing group to the song Addicted to Love, was the late Robert Palmer's most enduring image. He went on to become an icon of the '80s, with his slick style leading to much imitation. It was the high point in a career which had begun in the '60s as a teenager, when he joined the Alan Bown Set. This was followed by Vinegar Joe, alongside singer Elkie Brooks then after 3 successful L.Ps, Robert went solo.

With his impeccable suits and slicked-back hair, Robert had a hit with the Allen Toussaint song, Sneakin' Sally Through the Alley in 1974, which confirmed his status as a blue-eyed soul singer. Among the backing musicians on his 'Pressure Drop' album the following year were members of cult American band, Little Feat. A move to the Bahamas to record the L.Ps 'Double Fun' & 'Secrets' brought him success with singles 'Every Kinda People' and 'A Bad Case of Lovin' You'.

During 1982 Palmer had his biggest hit in Britain with Some Guys Have All the Luck then 3 years later had a side project, Power Station, teaming up with John & Andy Taylor of Duran Duran. The supergroup had 3 US Top 10 hits with Some Like It Hot, Communications and Get It On. Robert maintained this slick rock image in 'Addicted To Love' then 'I Didn't Mean To Turn You On', which offended some feminists but increased his popularity but he wasn't interested in the trappings of rock star fame: "I loved the music, but the excesses of rock music never really appealed to me at all. I couldn't see the point of getting up in front of a lot of people when you weren't in control of your wits".

Palmer moved with his family to Switzerland 16 years before he passed away, staying away from the celebrity limelight. He contributed to the movie 'Sweet Lies' before putting out 'Heavy Nova', which produced the hits, 'Simply Irresistible' & 'Early in the Morning'. His style became more varied, ranging from bossa nova to ballad crooning, having had a Top 10 hit, in collaboration with UB40, with Bob Dylan's 'I'll Be Your Baby Tonight' and the Marvin Gaye song, Mercy Mercy Me. The influence of African singer King Sunny Ade's music was clear on his album 'Honey' then a resurgent passion for the blues led to his L.P. 'Rhythm and Blues' [1999] followed by the album 'Drive', not long before he passed away, on which he played many of the instruments.

Embracing several musical genres over a long period & by eschewing the celebrity circus, Robert Palmer never had a huge following, but he was highly respected both for the songs that he sang, and the sincere, often understated way in which he sang them. Palmer was survived by Mary Ambrose, his partner of 20 years, along with his 2 children, Jim and Jane.

Robert Palmer sauntered into a restaurant in Milan, from 15 ft away looking almost exactly like he had a decade earlier when his visual style was as important as his musical substance. He was wearing the same sort of Armani designer suit, with that blank-eyed, bored expression that he'd had in his seminal '80s video 'Addicted To Love'. However, close-up there was something about the way the artist kept pulling down his waistcoat over his paunch that combined with the manner in which Robert was eyeing the menu to suggest that at 50 he may've become more addicted to Linguine than to love.

Palmer was there to discuss his 1st new L.P. for 5 years 'Rhythm & Blues', but by the time he'd started on the linguine he seemed happier to talk about his muse than his music. It seemed that his addiction to Mary Ambrose, with whom he'd lived for the previous 7-9 years, had led to the physical, emotional and musical changes in Robert. It was 35 year old Mary's cooking that had brought on the middle-age spread; it was her devotion that had made him happy and in good humour; while it was Ambrose's beauty & sensuality that had inspired him to create the softer, more romantic tracks on his latest album: "There's nothing more important to me than Mary. That's all there is. She's my reason for living. I write about love. Well, what else is there?"

During Palmer's career as a singer-songwriter, which had spanned over 30 years, encompassing hits including' Simply Irresistible', 'Mercy, Mercy Me', 'She Makes My Day' and Johnny & Mary - the theme for the Nicole and Papa ads - Robert had been circumspect about the women in his life. His 21-year marriage to ex-wife Sue, mother of his 2 kids, James 21 & Jane, 19, had been regarded as one of the most solid in the fickle, faithless music industry. At the height of his late-'80s fame and fortune he was a rare British rock star who strongly believed in family values.

Palmer took his wife & kids with him everywhere he went: "The kids had these Concorde books that were just full from all the times they flew with me". He shunned the groupies, along with other glamorous women that were part of his working life, including the beautiful clones in his 'Addicted To Love' video, having been the complete, faithful family man. Robert wouldn't discuss what happened at the end of their relationship;

"I never intended to change horses", but one believed him when he said that he'd been deeply upset by the break-up in 1991, so that even after he met Ambrose he'd been reluctant to get seriously involved: "It's beyond my dreams, my relationship, it's one of the first things in my life that has been. It's hard to express exactly what it is about her. We met in San Fransisco, where she was working as a waitress, which now I can see was a wonderful twist of fate. I fought it because it was the last thing in the world I wanted to happen. I resented her because I was obsessed with her but I wouldn't admit it".

When he did allow Mary into his life she changed hers, following him around the world like his former family had done. They lived as tax exiles in a converted mill house near Lake Lugano, Switzerland, 40 mins drive away from Milan, Italy. The exterior of their home was, "Hansel & Gretel", while the interior was stark, modern Milanese. The domestic nature of their relationship could be summed up by his intention, the previous Christmas, to buy Ambrose a BMW sports car, which she rejected, preferring a Gaggenau cooker.

Mary prepared the food which he ate; she nurtured, he created. No wonder he was so happy, living most men's ideal relationship, with a "voluptuous", submissive younger woman, who devoted much of her time to satisfying his needs: "Look, she doesn't hang on my coat-tails, she's very independent. I'm no Svengali. I mean, she gets bolshie, she won't put up with any nonsense, but she appreciates my point of view, because she respects my experience", Palmer said. Did he worry about Ambrose deciding that she'd like a baby or feeling that she might want her own career?

"Look she's a hedonist like me. She's the youngest of 6 children, so there isn't any biological clock ticking or some fantasy about babies or anything. She knows what kids involve. Besides, I don't think a child should have a 51 year old father. I've been there, done that at the right age when I was young. It's great with my kids. We get along really well, I'm very proud of them and they love Mary to pieces. Would I end the relationship if she was to pressurise me about kids? This is so theoretical as to be ludicrous. Actually, what she says is that I'm enough of a kid to look after. I know it's a frivolous remark, but it's probably true & if she did want a career then it took off, I'd follow her. I'd press her clothes, all that stuff, but she doesn't like the limelight". Ambrose was back at home in Lugano, doing the washing.

Later Robert posed for photos in the winter sunshine, pausing to look at a shoe shop window display that was dominated by the kind of sexy, 6-inch spiked stilletos that the models wore in 'Addicted To Love'. "That's why I love Italy. Every street is the same - a bar, a lingerie shop then a shoe shop. They've got their priorities right", Palmer grinned, as he leant moodily against a marble pillar outside Gucci for another snap.

Robert Palmer had 'never meant to turn us on' to the guitar-wielding girls in his 'Addicted to Love' video (1986), having come to rue discussing the hit that defined an era on MTV. The musician had never even danced with the sexy female band in his video, the girls being digitally edited into the final product, which wasn't Robert's idea: "It was a high-gloss fashion photographer — totally him. I'm delighted that the iconography he created is still valid, especially in the light of today's more overt vulgarity", Palmer said.

He'd long ago dismissed videos featuring girls flaunting big cleavage as "soft-core pornography", but trying to be philosophical about it, Robert also observed that his risqué videos and skinny-tie '80s persona were an undying public obsession. He'd had very different plans when he wrote 'Addicted to Love', having intended it to be a duet with Chaka Kahn. They recorded it, but her vocals were deleted when her manager barred the song's release.

Palmer and Khan had bumped into each other at a club when he was working on the song, as visions of a duet danced into his head, he said during 1986: "We hit it off immediately, I was impressed. She's the one singer I've always wanted to sing with". They went back to Robert's studio where they recorded together but the soul diva already had a couple of songs racing up the charts, so her managers didn't want to put too much product on the market.

However, the song leapt to the top of the charts, becoming Palmer's 1st Top 10 entry, while the video became an even bigger hit, making No. 8 on MTV's list of the 100 Greatest Videos Ever Made. Robert went on to become one of the most successful stars of the '80s, both as a solo artist & as the front man for Power Station, which he formed with Duran Duran heartthrobs John Taylor and Andy Taylor. Palmer's sudden success came as a surprise, even to his small cadre of hard-core fans, who weren't too impressed with his sudden turn to dance fluff. He'd earned his stripes as a blues rocker in the early '70s, opening for The Who & Jimi Hendrix as a member of Vinegar Joe.

Sneakin' Sally Through the Alley, his 1st solo album, received critical acclaim, Robert never really seeming concerned with carefully crafting his image, having once recorded a calypso version of the Kinks' hit, You Really Got Me'. Palmer had hung up his skinny ties years earlier, returning to the music of his younger days, performing a wide range of gospel, rhythm 'n' blues, and Caribbean funk but memories of the '80s lived on, so he had to answer for them: "I hardly ever get asked about music. However, I do get asked about the 'Addicted to Love' video & my suits on a daily basis". Robert, who may never have danced with that bevy of beauties, but had danced with questions about them ever since, said "They were all gorgeous. I did try to get a few phone numbers".

Meeting Robert Palmer could be an intimidating experience, with his pugnacious manager opening the door then leading one into a living room filled with folk - Palmer's son, daughter, wife, plus the man himself, looking dapper in brown leather shoes, with a blue Savile Row shirt. His look was only slightly ruffled by what appeared to be a wee tomato stain on his shoulder. Robert was sitting at a table, chain-smoking Dunhills, while downing a bottle of single-malt whisky. Yorkshire's most famous soul singer had matured into a handsome, apparently respectable middle-aged bloke with a raffish undertow.

Palmer's conversation was suggestive of an international lifestyle, with a studio in Milan, trips to LA, Rome, a house in Switzerland, although the glamour came at a price. "I hardly ever get asked about music. However, I do get asked about the 'Addicted to Love' video and my suits on a daily basis". The questions about '80s pop videos had come thick & fast over the previous few weeks, 'Robert Palmer at His Very Best', a CD collection that spanned his career, having just been issued, so while his evenings had been occupied by laying down new tracks at a studio in Hammersmith, Robert had spent his days "minding my Ps and Qs. You make one off-colour remark then that's all you hear about. I'm good at those".

Palmer was more complex than his slick image suggested. When he was 15 he joined his first band the Mandrakes, named in homage to William Burroughs's 'The Naked Lunch', his favourite book. "Required reading for the young hippy. It's the beauty of the prose that stuns me. 'A hail of crystal skulls falling slowly through a sky as clear & thick as glycerine.' What a fantastic image! Like a Dore etching". Robert paced around the room, animated by enthusiasm. "The Naked Lunch exists because somebody dug Burroughs out of the hole he was in, in Morocco. He hadn't left the room for weeks and he was a stinking mess, but there was paper everywhere, so they gathered it up then made it into a book."

Palmer took music that was important to him on the road, on top of the pile being a 24-track collection of bossa nova master Joao Gilberto's finest moments. "I like a lot of Brazilian music, but nothing has the intimate intensity that Gilberto is able to generate with his voice & guitar. It's so sophisticated. You can whistle his songs, but try to learn how to play one. It'll take you a year". Gilberto was a private man, so much so that his daughter Bebel had complained of not being allowed in the same room as him. He'd turned eccentric with age, reputedly living in solitude at his Rio home plus a series of hotel rooms, Robert being one of the privileged few to have been granted an audience with him:

"I was eating in a restaurant in Milan when this guy tapped me on the shoulder. It was Gilberto's son, who said that as he'd had heard I was a big fan of his dad's, would I like to see his concert in Rome? So we went, it was wonderful. I remember a Learjet passing the crescent moon as he played this delicious piece of music. Gilberto's son invited us back to the hotel. I'm with my son and my daughter, when we walked in to see Gilberto wearing sunglasses. He didn't say a word. My son Jim said to me: 'My God, it's like meeting Brando!' For some reason I mentioned pot, as his eyes lit up then all of a sudden I was his new best friend. It turned out that he was a big stoner, so before I knew it I was being invited back to his house in Rio".

While Otis Redding, Marvin Gaye & Wilson Pickett became Palmer's heroes as a teenager, being the reason that he'd started singing in the 1st place, he'd grown up with the music of Gilberto and Nat King Cole in Malta, where his father was stationed in the Navy. "He had perfect pitch. He could start singing while a 36-piece orchestra joined in seamlessly & he didn't embellish the songs. I think it was because he was such an excellent piano player - he knew exactly where the notes should fall," Robert said of Cole's appeal.

He picked up CDs as he passed through countries, Terence Trent d'Arby, who'd changed his name to Sananda Maitreya after receiving an instruction in a dream, having given Palmer his latest L.P. He'd also just bought Damon Albarn's collaboration with musicians from Mali - "I'd give you my copy, but it's for Oxfam, so buy it yourself" - along with a CD of the 8-fingered gypsy guitarist Django Reinhardt's solo recordings, of whom he said "It's his skill that astounds me. He doesn't cover a huge range, but it's exact, yet you never feel that he's staring at his fingers with his tongue sticking out of his mouth. He was a genius, there aren't many of them".

Viewing Dizzee Rascal's latest video, one could argue that it was part of a full-scale revival of the Addicted to Love treatment. Folk had enjoyed the flashy brass, along with big, hammering drums, plus the tension and swagger in Robert's voice, with the frisson of release on the chorus, "Might as well face it...". Fans also liked the video's mannequin-like female backing group, all with hard, unsmiling faces & chic, monochrome curves, although Addicted to Love was a rather like the Police's Every Step You Take, being a song one enjoyed until old enough to re-evaluate the lyrics.

Palmer thought that he knew the girl of the song's gaze better than she knew herself – that he could sense great, untapped reserves of desire hidden behind her mask of primness, believing that he'd liberate her with his manly intuition and physical prowess. If that sounded familiar it could be because Robin Thicke's 'Blurred Lines', the song that had launched many angry-brilliant-rubbish parodies by enraged feminists and clever queers, was Addicted to Love reborn. Why hadn't someone made a mashup?

Songs with the lyrics 'You like to think that you're immune to the stuff' & 'Another kiss is all you need', like Thicke's 'but you're a good girl', 'Just let me liberate you,' were part of a tradition that operated in a morally grey area, sitting between praising women who acquiesced to their repressed, carnal desires and bragging about 'good girls' who surrendered to their inner sluts when faced with the artist's supreme, overwhelming, stud masculinity.

The latter idea was perhaps insulting, because it robbed the female protagonists of any real autonomy 'Your mind is not your own', although the kernel of truth in those songs was that: women lived in a world that objectified and oversexualised their bodies then shamed them when they dared to take back control & sexual agency. The anti-porn, sex-negative feminist brigade were partly to blame for perpetuating the predicament, something 'Savages' singer Jehnny Beth had discussed earlier that year. 'Although Beth agrees with the feminist movement's aims for equality, she has misgivings about its wider motivations, being fascinated when women put a feminist reading on Savages':

"They tell me they think pornography is bad for women and assume I'm going to understand. The thing is, I watch a lot of pornography. It's been very important for me, to liberate myself from the pressure of romanticism, the myth of a woman's pleasure". They'd been taught that they needed men's gaze, prompting & permission to enjoy themselves, which was the tension that Thicke exploited in Blurred Lines. Some females thought that the song was 'rape-y', the video not being easy to defend, with the nudity of its girl stars but not their male co-stars being problematic, along with its suggestion that a woman's sexuality was purely base and primal - 'You're an animal, baby it's in your nature' - while Robin's was presumably more sophisticated.

One could also take offence at the infantile language and props, including a rocking horse but Blurred Lines was a mutual dance: 'The way you grab me/Must wanna get nasty/Go ahead, get at me'. Even if Thicke's indulgent, self-congratulatory display of playa masculinity was over the top, being full of misogynist images, the topic of consent in Blurred Lines was explicit. Consent was central to Dizzee's song, despite the title codifying casual sex as 'bad'. Unlike the smug, pseudo-knowingness and predatory vibes in Robert Palmer's hit, Dizzee's love interest was an independent, sexually empowered woman, out to get kicks on her own terms.

He was both bowled over & impressed by her frankness, framing their tryst as shame-free 'That's ok / ain't gotta explain / nothing wrong with sharing love, its just an exchange'. However, like Robin, Dizzee was also a victim of the good girl/bad girl trap: 'And I know you're not a hoe, you don't usually play / you would never just leave, you would usually stay / never have a one-night stand'. At times, the gals in the video for 'Something Really Bad' stared at the camera face-on, like they were squaring up. Blurred Lines director Diane Martel employed the same technique:

"I wanted to deal with the misogynist, funny lyrics in a way where the girls were going to overpower the men. Look at Emily Ratajkowski's performance; it's very, very funny & subtly ridiculing. That's what's fresh to me. It also forces the men to feel playful, not at all like predators. I directed the girls to look into the camera, that's very intentional, they do it most of the time; they're in the power position".

Martel believed that the peacock egotism in Blurred Lines was explicit enough to tip the sexism over into self-ridicule, having had a point. Who could take a guy who used inflatable balloons to increase his penis size seriously? Whether or not one agreed with Martel, the idea that women needed men to liberate them, or give them permission to engage in the joys of promiscuous, carefree sex, was played out.

Love had been Robert Palmer's affliction during 1979 with a 'Bad Case of Loving You', but it had turned into a more serious problem by 1986, having become 'Addicted to Love', the 2nd single on his Riptide album. The song had originally been conceived as a duet with Chaka Kahn until her label, Warner Bros., refused to let her sing on the track, so Robert had to re-record the high notes himself. A few more guys rounded out the instrumentation, including his Power Station bandmate Andy Taylor, of Duran Duran, on guitar, but the song wasn't without female influence.

Palmer was backed by a 'group' of lookalike model girls who were little more than fashionable accessories for the suave singer. Indeed, looks trumped musical ability when director Terence Donovan had auditioned them for the clip: "I was 21 when I got the part on the strength of my modelling book. We were meant to look and 'act' like showroom mannequins," said Mak Gilchrist, the 'bassist'. The quartet had struck a dramatic image in their little black dresses, Donovan, a British fashion photographer known for capturing the mod fashion of the Swinging '60s, having shifted his lens to the '80s.

Terence completed the Palmer Girl look with slicked-back hair, rouged cheekbones, and red-glossed lips, to create an iconic slice of '80s fashion that made the video accompanying the driving, sensual song 'Addicted To Love' unforgettable, confirming that the increasingly popular music video medium could have a powerful effect on a song's success, as the single shot to the top of the charts. However, not everyone was pleased with the trend of using girls as props, feminist critics accusing Robert of sexism and 'sexploitation'. "I was as much a prop as the girls," he countered, having brought back Donovan with a bevy of Palmer Girls for his acclaimed 'Simply Irresistible' video in 1988.

Many artists paid homage to both clips, with Paula Abdul recruiting wee lassies to emulate the Palmer Girls in her 'Forever Your Girl' video & Shania Twain doing a gender flip with a crew of male models in 'Man! I Feel Like a Woman!' Pepsi promoted their 'simply irresistible' soft drink with a parody of the video during 1989 then again in 2002 with Britney Spears. The 21st century continued to push the envelope towards objectification with increasingly provocative videos casting girls as sex objects, leading to discussions about misogyny in music.

The 'Addicted to Love' video, featuring deadpan, mini-skirted models dispassionately playing instruments behind the handsome Robert Palmer, became one of MTV's most heavily rotated music videos, while sparking feminist protests. "These women were put in after I finished filming, and I've had to live them down ever since," Robert said in 1994. Black-clad bombshells had shown up again in his music videos for 'I Didn't Mean to Turn You On' and 'Simply Irresistible'. Palmer was known for his understated vocals & eclectic musical tastes, his L.P. 'Don't Explain'(1990) including R&B, jazz, reggae and pre-'50s torch songs, as well as a couple of rockers. 'You get the feeling that he merely tolerates the rockers because their mass appeal allows him to sing what he really wants to sing -- the quirky, quaint, vintage pop songs he really loves', wrote one reviewer..

The artist was known as a man who knew how to dress -- his sartorial role models as a performer haing been the immaculate Marvin Gaye & Otis Redding. Palmer's GQ sense of style had led Rolling Stone magazine, which once dismissed him as 'white soul for snobs', to name him the best-dressed male artist of 1990. Although Robert's good looks and dapper suits were a strong attraction for his female fans at concerts, the focus on his looks irritated him:

"It would get on my nerves. The media made it worse. They didn't know much about my music, so they dealt with these other superficial things, but it's not so much of a problem any more. Now I have hit records they can talk about," he said during 1986. "My parents were part of a crowd that was attached to all the different navies stationed in Malta. When they'd have parties in each other's houses, I'd get taken along, so that's where I heard all this great music. I didn't distinguish particular styles; it was all music to me" he recalled in 1994.

Palmer told Rolling Stone magazine, "I'm not concerned that my stuff isn't extreme. I don't want to be heavy. I can't think of another attitude to have toward an audience than a hopeful, positive one, and if that includes such unfashionable things as sentimentality, well, I can afford it". Robert, who was best known for his sharp suits & for creating an iconic pop video, attributed his distinctive voice to his chain-smoking and liking for malt whisky. His heavy smoking & appreciation of single malt was well known, but the obituarist damned Palmer with faint praise.

He was a pop star of the '80s - '90s, whose success came after over a decade 'paying his dues' as a hard-working singer, touring with rock, blues and soul bands. Robert joined rock fusion group Dada, which became Vinegar Joe, on rhythm guitar while sharing vocals with the dynamic Elkie Brooks, known for their electrifying live performances on the UK concert circuit. Brooks said that she and the other members of Vinegar Joe used alcohol & cocaine to combat exhaustion on their hectic touring schedules. She later also acquired a taste for Scotch: 'My favourite tipple is Glenmorangie whisky,' she stated after becoming a successful solo artist. '

With success during the '80s came the legend of Palmer as a chain-smoking whisky drinker, journalists reporting that he'd turn up for interviews with a pack of Dunhills and a bottle of single malt, steadily working his way through both during the day. However, there were no tales of wild, drunken excess, Robert having been courteous & accommodating in his dealings with the press, being committed to behaving and drinking responsibly while working.

When Andy Taylor of Duran Duran went to see him before a gig in Japan, he spotted a bottle of single malt on his dressing room table but Palmer refused to open it, concerned about the effect drinking would have on his voice & performance if he indulged before going on stage. However, the singer was happy to let his hair down after he'd finished his set; Taylor recalling that the pair drank the whisky after the concert, before embarking on a tour of Tokyo's bars and clubs that didn't end until 10.30am the following day.

Robert moved to Lugano, Switzerland in 1993, acquiring a much-admired wine cellar, having lived happily there until he died suddenly in Paris at the age of 54, after suffering a massive heart attack. There were suggestions that a rock 'n' roll lifestyle might have played a role in his early death, but he'd been given a clean bill of health following a check-up just weeks earlier. It was only after his death that his partner Mary Ambrose revealed that Palmer had a secret addiction, stating that he'd leave her alone in bed at night while he indulged in his greatest passion – building model trucks and aeroplanes downstairs.

5 years into his solo career, Robert Palmer had already covered more musical ground than many artists travelled in a lifetime but he'd only just begun, as demonstrated by the issue of his 5th album, 'Secrets', in June 1979. After departing the unjustly overlooked R&B group Vinegar Joe during 1974, Palmer struck out on his own with Sneakin' Sally Through the Alley, a funk-rich L.P. cut with members of the Meters and Lowell George of Little Feat, with a sound that spilled over into the albums that followed, although he was clearly restless.

From 'Pressure Drop' (1975) to 'Some People Can Do What They Like' [1976] then Double Fun (1978), Robert included everything from reggae to hard rock and disco, having a musically expansive approach that may've disappointed listeners hoping for a sequel to Sneakin' Sally Through the Alley, but one that befitted a peripatetic lifestyle, as his family moved from the U.K. to New York then The Bahamas. 'Secrets' was surprising, because rather than delving deeper into new territory it had a relatively narrow focus, Palmer concentrating on the rock side of his sound with covers including Moon Martin's 'Bad Case of Loving You (Doctor, Doctor)' & Todd Rundgren's 'Can We Still Be Friends'.

Both became Robert's signature singles, but he thought that any hit potential was mainly an accident, saying in 1976, "I believe that my music is just about feelings and the style is just a side effect. I get really bored with style. I'm sick to death of it. Just style as a commodity, whether it's disco or heavy metal or whatever the current trend is. I mean, I'm just really bored with it, always have been. For instance, I used to do a lot of reggae tunes – or things in that area – but now if I do them folk come up to me saying, 'You're jumping on the ska bandwagon'. I just get sick of it".

Palmer went on to state that he enjoyed making L.Ps that confounded anyone's preconceived expectations: "I don't want to make an album where it's presumed I'm into something. I mean, I haven't got a band, I never have had. I've got to the point where I just get on with it, with the content of what I put on the records being determined from what I learn from the audience, from what works live, from what I want to hear when I go to a club or what I'd like to play when I get home. I'm just trying to include all those different things, mixing it up, because otherwise you end up with, what do they call it, a 'concept' L.P. or something".

Although Robert may've appreciated that he could count on his own growing following of fans, his eclectic style was also partly motivated by a less loyal form of listening: "I'm only interested in, I only like songs. There's no groups or singers that I like at all. I like songs by a lot of different folk, but I'm certainly not a fan of anybody. I make up cassettes all the time – to take on the road with me – a song from this album, a song from that L.P. That's the way I listen to music; it's like one of those K Tel things, it's from all over. I listen to Fred Astaire, I listen to African folk music, I listen to Talking Heads".

At times in his career that song-1st focus had hindered Palmer's career as much as it helped it, as although forward-thinking sides like his cover of Gary Numan's 'I Dream of Wires' [1980] or his take on the R&B duo 'The System's' song 'You Are In My System' [1983] were usually warmly received by critics, it made him a hard artist to promote. After 'Riptide' [1985], produced by Bernard Edwards of Chic, took Robert to multi-platinum mainstream success, left turns like his standards-driven Don't Explain album [1990] risked alienating a much broader audience.

However, with Secrets [1979], he began a period of mid-level hit singles, as following on from the Top 20 entry of his Double Fun cut 'Every Kinda People', he repeated the feat with 'Bad Case of Loving You', continuing to nibble at the airwaves on either side of the Atlantic throughout the early part of the decade. By the time he joined up with the all-star Chic/Duran Duran mash-up 'the Power Station' during 1984, Palmer had carved out an impressive musical niche for himself without ever really basking in the spotlight, which was just as he liked it:

"I joined a band because I didn't like school and there's nothing else I'd rather have done. If I really wanted to make money I'd be in real estate, but I'm comfortably well-off. I have a son & daughter, a lovely home, and if I see something I like I can buy it. That's rich enough". Robert later stated that he wasn't "trying to build an audience or create a market or product. I'm trying to make up songs that I like to sing then put them on a record, be pleased with the result, saying, 'Yeah, I've made the best record I could make this year'. I'll leave it up to someone else to market it. Of course, it does give me problems. You can't be easily categorized; folk tend to concentrate on my appearance, which is kind of frustrating". As he'd soon find out, thanks to the video-driven image he'd unleash with Riptide, people concentrating on appearance could be even more annoying than he'd any way of knowing at the time, but in 1979, Palmer's Secrets were still safe.

Robert Palmer's 'Addicted to Love', which had topped the Billboard Hot 100 thirty-five years ago, was best known for its brilliantly idiotic video, featuring him performing in front of 5 stunning mannequin-like models, with vapid facial expressions, holding musical instruments that they were not even pretending to mime convincingly. They couldn't dance either, only occasionally moving in time with the song's rhythm. It was utterly ridiculous, Robert's face in the video showing that he knew it, but absolutely iconic at the same time.

There was little question that the Terence Donovan-directed visual eye-worm played a pivotal role in driving the song, which was originally released 6 months earlier on Palmer's 'Riptide' album, to No. 1 on the chart dated May 3rd, 1986, knocking Prince and the Revolution's 'Kiss' from the top spot for a week, before giving way to the Pet Shop Boys' 'West End Girls'. The video was oddly unforgettable, leading to many imitations, along with whatever passed for memes during the mid-'80s, so much so that it overshadowed the song, which was in a league of brilliant stupidity all of its own.

Any songwriter worth their salt could tell you that a certain degree of simplicity was half the battle, as after all, what good was art that no one wanted to see or hear? Also, clearly the brilliant musicians that producer Bernard Edwards assembled for 'Addicted to Love', a song of Neanderthal-level simplicity, understood that. The song was built around an A-G-D-A chord progression that could be played on 2 guitar strings, but like the video, was nevertheless almost impossible to get out of one's head & although the musicians did manage to slip in some sly licks, in the parlance of the era, they checked their egos in at the door when serving up the song.

Holding down the all-important beat was the Chic rhythm section, with Edwards on bass and Tony Thompson on drums, the same guys who'd inadvertently built the foundation of hip-hop when the rhythm track of Chic's 'Good Times' was incorporated into Sugarhill Gang's hit 'Rapper's Delight' [1979], the first widely popular rap song. Tony, who also worked with Chic co-founder Nile Rodgers on David Bowie's 'Let's Dance' L.P., played a thwacking 2-4 rhythm, showing off with an open hi-hat flourish on the 3 that gave the song one of its key hooks, cranked up to booming volume in the way that only '80s drums could be, making it crunch even harder by playing as far behind the beat as humanly possible. Bernard made this slow & very stompy song dance, with a simple but amazingly funky bass-line that anchored the riff, while also making it elastic, his bass-line dancing exponentially better than the models in the video.

That grinding guitar riff was the centre of the song. While Duran Duran's Andy Taylor contributed a squalling, impressively dumb solo at the end, the main riff came from Eddie Martinez, who played the screaming guitars on Run-DMC's ground-breaking rap-metal anthem 'Rock Box' [1984]." Keyboardist Wally Badarou, who not only worked with Grace Jones and Herbie Hancock but played the stunning synthesizer solos on Talking Heads' 'Burning Down the House' & 'This Must Be the Place', brought those sweeping keyboard hooks and the subtle, skittering sequencer that underpinned the song's rhythm.

Finally, there was Robert himself, the song's sole credited writer, who was one of the best British R&B singers of his generation but kept it relatively low-key here, delivering a suave, soulful vocal that, on the chorus, he practically turned into a percussion instrument - 'Ah-dick-tid-to-love'. Even his outfit in the video conveyed restraint: Wearing a starched white shirt, black tie and high-waisted black pants, he looked like a businessman whose idea of casual was taking off his jacket.

Palmer hadn't intended to sing by himself, 'Addicted to Love' having been recorded as a duet with R&B icon Chaka Khan, but her vocal being dropped before the song was issued. Robert was none too pleased by that development: "Politics intervened," the "seething" singer said in 1986. "Her people said it was a conflict of interest. She'd have 3 singles out at the same time". However, she did get a credit for the vocal arrangement. "She threw parts in and helped develop the song. I couldn't use her vocals but she deserves credit for what she contributed to the arrangement". While several Palmer-Khan duets were on YouTube, sadly, 'Addicted to Love' wasn't one of them but the hugely talented Khan didn't really do stupid, so without hearing the song it was hard to say how in on the joke she may've been.

Although Palmer had worked with a wide range of musicians during his career, from the Meters to Little Feat, this unusual combination was probably the single best thing to come from the Power Station, the slightly odious 'super-group' comprised of Robert, Edwards, Thompson, Andy Taylor and his Duran Duran bandmate John Taylor that took its name from the famous New York Studio, releasing a rather dreadful but commercially successful album during 1985, led by a bilious cover of T. Rex's 'Bang a Gong (Get It On)'.

The musicians had intended to work with a variety of singers, but hit it off with Palmer so well that they did the entire, hastily recorded L.P. with him. However, he turned down the chance to join an equally hastily organized tour & appearance at Live Aid to work on 'Riptide', but most of the musicians reunited for 'Addicted to Love', showing none of the restraint on 'The Power Station' that they did on 'Addicted', Tony show-boating all over the album.

Unfortunately, the key individuals involved in the song weren't able to talk about any of this: Bernard and Terence having died in 1996 then Robert & Thompson passing away within a couple of months of each other during 2003. However, the song, the video and their influence remained, having been referenced in a Britney Spears Pepsi advert 10 years earlier, which for musicians, was proof of the importance of serving the song. 'Addicted to Love', was so effective because it was performed by top-flight musicians not over-thinking it, just giving the song what it required. Like so many AC/DC songs, it sounded simple, but it wasn't at all.

Was it brilliantly idiotic or idiotically brilliant? Of course, it was both: No less a connoisseur of brilliant idiocy than Slade front-man Noddy Holder, the man responsible for such classics as 'Cum on Feel the Noize' & 'Mama Weer All Crazee Now' said: "The one main song that I wish that I'd written and recorded is 'Addicted to Love' by Robert Palmer. To me, that's a perfect pop song". It was hard to think of a more shining example of the oft-quoted line from another iconic piece of art from the era, 'This Is Spinal Tap': "It's such a fine line between stupid and clever".

"'Respect' by Otis Redding was the 1st piece of music that totally engulfed my attention, as I started to collect records. I wrote to Stax, Atlantic, Motown & Sun Records, while discovering things like the British label,' Sue', that issued ska singles. It was more than a minor obsession! It led me into the pursuit of atmosphere in music, something completely different from what other folk were into at the time. Everybody else was playing Yardbirds and Chuck Berry, while I was doing the 'Harlem Shuffle'.

I used to hate it when I was in my first group in Yorkshire, we'd open for The Move & Jimi Hendrix and I'd think, 'How come these people act that way? What gives them the right to be that way?' I still can't understand.

I can waste less words now, people understand me more quickly. It just hits quicker. The enthusiasm I'm getting is matching my enthusiasm for the projects, instead of having to fire a situation to get what I want, it's coming right at me...

I've been playing music for 12 years and I don't want to make a mistake, because I'm making my shot now, but I've been taking my time doing it, because there are so many easy routes which look so treacherous to me that I ain't prepared to tread 'em. I enjoy singing; it's the only thing I do that gives me complete satisfaction & I don't want to jeopardise that.

Allen Toussaint was hanging around the studio when we were making Sneakin' Sally Through The Alley, but Steve Smith was the producer. The Meters are a burning band, they lock together like a musical puzzle. If you listen to any individual part, it seems so simple. It's African, it's all about syncopation.

I've bought a house in Nassau. I'm off there in a couple of days. It's the 1st place I've had to live since last August when I left England. I wasn't staying anywhere more than a month, and it was beginning to get to me, having nowhere to hang your toothbrush, y'know. It's right by the sea, I can go to check out the tropical fish.

I can buy myself a house in Nassau & I can afford to fly back and forth, fly my wife back & forth, and go to see my parents, fly them out for Christmas & stuff like that. They're the things I really like to do, and I get to be able to do them because I like to sing. That seems really precious to me, so I don't want to jeopardise it.

Home in Nassau is very, very quiet, it's neutral ground. It's a place where there's no competition & no structures. It takes away a lot of the false class crap you find here, where folk look at your shoes or listen to your accent then slot you.

This new L.P. 'Some People Can Do What They Like' is a killer, it really is. It's nice because I don't need to feel awkward when people come up to me to say they really like my stuff. I can say, 'Thank you very much, that's what I do & I do it to the best of my ability. I like it too.

I had a radio hit in America. So I just came over. I just followed the demand rather than trying to go places to create one. That's why it took me so long to get back to England. I like to go places I'm asked, instead of inviting folk to come to see if they like it: 'Did I pass the audition?' I'd had enough of that in the groups I was in in England.

I pursue music like I relate to a woman. I feel the rhythm 1st, then the melody, and finally the lyric. I want to turn into a dolphin next time around. They are the hippest creatures on earth. They appear to have more intelligence than humans, more sensory potential, yet they spend their time in play.

Personally, I've always thought that making hit records was a useless pursuit in itself. I'd rather build an audience gradually, creating a demand myself rather than use the music industry machinery to create that demand.

James Jamerson, what a fabulous fellow. 5 ft 3", never changed his strings & when he'd find a line – because his lines were like songs themselves – he'd stop the take. He'd get so high on himself, he'd go 'Listen, listen! I've found it!'

I'd rather visit a place then play to the demand I've already created, so that it's realistic and I understand the audience reaction. They're not just clapping because everybody else is. So in some places we play 200-seat clubs for 3 nights, 2 shows a night. Other places we go in to do one show to 3,000 folk then go out of the place. It just depends what's happening in each place.

I was doing 3 of Gary Numan's tunes in my live show c. 18 months ago, who came to see the show with his dad. We got on really well so I suggested that...well, actually he suggested that we work together, so we did.

People either love what I do or hate what I do – so I've got to the point where I just get on with it & the content of what I put on the records is determined from what I learn from the audience, from what works live, from what I want to hear when I go to a club or what I'd like to play when I get home.

I'm just trying to include all those different things and mix it up, 'cos otherwise you end up with, what do they call it, a 'concept' album or something...

Lowell George was extremely bright, with a surreal sort of wit, and he was basically a workaholic. Day & night, all he did was make music. I'd never met him until we met up in New Orleans, but it was just instant. After the first couple of songs, he said 'I've got this group, howzabout you come to sing with my band?' So I joined up with Little Feat then went on the road with them for 6 months.

When I read about myself in the papers, I'm fascinated. I don't know what they're talking about... it's just journalists and record companies trying to create an image for me. Sure, I like food, clothes & the company of women...but a sophisticate and a womanizer? Give me a break!

I always find it very difficult to pinpoint any one particular Marvin Gaye song...It's the mood he creates when he goes into it, like that 'I Want You' record, it's just a gas, but I never went to see Marvin Gaye sing live, because I didn't want to see him take his shirt off & all that stuff.

My manager always accuses me of being a cruiser – he says I cruise through things, whereas he believes in going at them with your fists, but I don't have that kind of pride. The only things I believe in are birth and death, in between you get on with it".

Robert Palmer wore sharp suits, surrounding himself with impossibly svelte models, while apparently detesting discussing any aspect of his charmed existence with the media. The ex-pat Yorkshireman wrote great songs, having straddled musical genres when Puff Daddy was still Puff Baby, but took himself too seriously; he wouldn't have known self-deprecation if it had sat on his 5-year-old-face. It seemed strange then, to find him nursing a Martini in his London hotel, a picture of bonhomie, keen to introduce his beautiful but resolutely unsvelte American girlfriend, Mary Ambrose: "I've been trying to work out where I got this reputation for not liking the press. I don't know. I probably got one idiot trying to corner me at a really busy time, so bit his head off. Next thing I know I'm an embittered old recluse".

Palmer lived close to the Swiss-Italian border, having a jet-set lifestyle but all the other popular preconceptions were little truer than his alleged disdain for the Forth Estate. "I really love nice clothes, but so would you if you lived near Milan. The thing about decent tailoring is that it insulates you against the vagaries of fashion. There aren't any pictures of me in daft trousers or silly hats that can get dragged up when someone wants to make me look a prat".

His latest ensemble of a natty gaberdine jacket with triple-pleted trousers, Italian silk tie, white shirt with razor sharp collar and a dark wool, high-buttoning waistcoat, contributed to his over-earnest reputation: "I look like Little Lord Fauntleroy," he rasped in a cigarette-tainted voice that combined Batley bluntness with Eurotrash drawl & West Coast slang. With the manufactured persona of Addicted To Love, the smash that out-smoothed Miami Vice, changing the face of modern videos, so comprehensively dismantled, we were left with just the music, which suited Robert just fine.

Robert had a new single, 'True Love', being issued the following day, with an album of striking Soul-based grooves, 'Rhythm And Blues', due out the next month. It was the work of a man steeped in his art, just how deeply being shown by the way his craggy features lit up when he discussed its traditions & history: "Did you know that Nat King Cole became a singer by accident?" he asked after Mary prompted him to share what was clearly a favourite story. "He was pianist in a band but the singer got ill just before a TV appearance, so all the others said he had to sing because he was the most junior member. He hated it and that's why his arrangements are so special. He puts the piano's voice before his own".

This beguiling blend of gossip and artistic insight was the essence of the man, who lived & breathed music, displaying a breathtaking, decidedly un-English open-mindedness that led him to the strangest places. "One of my favourite records in years is Brandy's 'Never Say Never', he said, unconcerned that ageing rockers weren't expected to name-check pubescent popsters. "I look at the American R'n'B charts and, for the first time in years, see artists crossing boundaries but retaining consistency in a way that excites me".

The highly unimaginative title of his latest L.P. 'Rhythm And Blues', shouldn't have led listeners to draw conclusions over Palmer's bid to muscle in on similar turf. "Do you know what the term means? To some folk it's Otis Redding territory, to others it's the Motown sound but now it's Monica and Brandy. I looked it up in a music dictionary, which states "An American form with the emphasis on the backbeat" and that's what I like about it. It lets me explore melody & chords in a fairly conventional way but I can do it over African rhythm or whatever I like. I wanted to jettison my trademark shotgun approach. You know, one song was Bossa Nova, the next Heavy Metal, I wanted to make an album which you could put on then leave. I hope I have".

He had, but his greatest enthusiasm was reserved for discussing someone else's music. "My son James has just started out," he said, after a couple of bottles of Pinot Grigio and a brace of post-prandial Scotches had dismantled what remained of his "massive shyness". Robert continued, "He's an excellent musician - drums, bass, guitar, the works - but his real strength's writing & whatever happens in this business that's always going to be the most important thing". Following an impromptu rendition of one of James's latest compositions, the conversation turned to starrier collaborations, illuminating the steel behind Palmer's affable exterior.

"There won't be any more Power Station stuff", he said of the super-group that he'd assembled with ex-Chic bassist Bernard Edwards and Duran Duran's Andy Taylor. "Mary's got great empathy with Andy but I think he needs to practise more, when Bernard died, the group seemed to have run its course". Had the bassist's premature death from acute pneumonia made it hard to recapture motivation? "It wasn't that. Quite frankly the drummer, Tony Thompson, lacked discipline. Bernard used to keep him in check but I didn't have the time, energy or inclination to do so. He's selling seat-belts in Saudi-Arabia now".

It was this professionalism, combined with an impatience with anyone less committed that had kept Robert near the top of the pop tree since the '70s. His hunger remained & with it came an appetite for new developments that should've seen him stay there. He then spoke of different hunger: "You'll never guess what I ate the other night," laughed the guy with a reputation for staying as tightly-buttoned as his trademark suits. "I had roast oig and chocolate. It was .... Oooh.... Wow!...... Amazing!" A combination every bit as beautiful as the timeless twinning of rhythm 'n' blues?

'I'm gonna have to face it, I'm addicted to finding then interviewing pop culture fixtures who've rarely if ever been interviewed before, being particularly pumped about this entry in the '80s music video series, because it's the 1st article ever to include all 5 original Palmer Girls from 'Addicted to Love': From left to right when watching the video:

Julie Pankhurst (keyboard)
Patty Elias (Patty Kelly) (guitar)
Kathy Davies (drums)
Mak Gilchrist (bass)
Julia Bolino (guitar)

Patty and Julia got wed during the summer of 2013, the former having been hardest to find. Julie had not been in touch recently but had a lead, which luckily panned out, enabling a complete set, achieving the first virtual reunion of what could be the most visually memorable 'band' in music video history.

How old were they when they appeared in the 'Addicted to Love' video?

Julie: "21".

Patty: "I believe that the video was shot in 1985. Could have been '84. You can confirm. I was 18 in 1984". [The video came out in 1986, so 20 then].

Kathy: "24".

Mak: "21".

Julia: "19".

Where were they living at the time?

Julie: "London".

Patty: "I was living in London, a model with Models 1 on the Kings Road".

Kathy: "I was living in Hampstead with another model friend. I grew up in South Kensington.

Mak: "Paris & London".

Julia: "London".

Patty was the only American of the 5. Where had she grown up?

Patty: "I grew up through my pre-teens in Deer Park, Long Island then my family moved to Longmont, Colorado to try 'ranching'. I left home for Tokyo aged 17, the day after I graduated from high school".

What music videos, shows, or movies had they appeared in before that?

Julie: "None, eeks, what was that about 'not one-line answers'…?"

Patty: "This was the early period in music video history. Truth be told, I didn't know what a music video was. I'd been living in Europe, not watching much television, so I didn't know about MTV or music videos".

Kathy: "I was in the video for 'Figures' by Zaine Griff [the woman who walked straight at the camera close to the beginning of the video] and also one directed by Paul McCartney, a Jamaican reggae group called the Simeons; I honestly don't remember the name. I was also in Octopussy, just another Bond girl".

Mak: "I'd done plenty of commercials".

Julia: "A Rod Stewart video & one ('All the Love in the World') for a group named The Outfield".

Kathy, what had it been like to work with Paul McCartney?

Kathy: "Great. It was a family affair, as Linda came to the studio with the kids. He was incredibly charming and kind. He was very relaxed, making everyone feel comfortable".

How were they cast?

Julie: "I'd just joined Models 1 model agency & Terence Donovan held a casting at his studio. He based his decision on looks and persona".

Patty: "I was also cast by Terence Donovan and I believe that I was the prototype for the casting. Terence & I had shot several ads for Neutrogena, so he was familiar with me and the way I looked on film".

Kathy: "Strangely, I didn't go to any casting. I was just booked direct at the agency".

Mak: "I didn't go to a casting either. I was known to the director, Terence Donovan, who booked me direct via my agent".

Julia: "A normal casting with the director Terence Donovan; they looked at my portfolio then took a Polaroid pic".

Could they remember what their reaction was when they were cast?

Julie: "Being a model was very new to me, so every booking was a great adventure. To work with one of our legendary photographers so soon gave me positive vibes for the potential of my career".

Patty: "My reaction was 'total bliss'. I was young & game for anything, especially anything that Terence Donovan was working on. Everything he did at the time was magic".

Kathy: "I was very excited when I heard that I'd be working with Terence Donovan again and making a video".

Mak: "I had no idea then what this video would become. It was just another booking, except this one was with someone whose music I liked. I wasn't easily starstruck".

Julia: "I'd never heard of Robert Palmer at the time, as I think I was more into funk bands, so not overly excited!"

Kathy, why was she assigned to be the drummer?

Kathy: "I guess the naughty ones always get sent to the back!"

Had it bothered her that she was blocked by Robert for most of the video?

Kathy: "Not really. He had a good bum".

Where was the video filmed & how long was the shoot?

Julie: "It was a very small production in the depths of Holborn Studios, in central London. The shoot took a day and Donovan liked to work in a relaxed manner, so it was a very chilled day. Prep in the morning (hair, make-up & styling) followed by a long lazy lunch then Robert Palmer arrived for the filming".

Patty: "The video was shot in a studio in London. I don't remember where, but I remember that the tea cart always rolled in about 3 in the afternoon. Union, I think! I believe that the shoot was either 3 days or 5...probably 3".

Mak: "Holborn Studios in Back Hill, London, in a basement, in just 1 day".

Julia: "It was filmed in Holborn Studios, sadly now closed. It took a day. We started at 8:00 a.m., finishing at c. 7pm".

Was the shoot the 1st time that they'd met each other?

Julie: "I may've met Patty and Mak at 'Models 1' but most probably at the casting, because the shoot was just after I'd joined the agency. I met Julia and Kathy at the shoot".

How had they felt making the video?

Julie: "It wasn't every day that we got to be involved in a pop video, so the whole experience was great fun".

Patty: "Since I'd never seen a music video before, I was unsure of what was going on. We spent many hours in make-up then we'd come out when the music would start. It really felt quite experimental".

Kathy: "It was a great day. We all had a lot of fun & there was a terrific atmosphere".

Mak: "Hmmm, well, the make-up was transforming, I barely recognized myself. The other girls and creative team were all lovely, so there was a great vibe. I didn't feel nervous. I was working hard at that stage, so took it in my stride".

Julia: "It was a really fun day. I got to pretend to be a stroppy lead guitarist!"

What was the most difficult part of the shoot?

Julie: "Keyboards...playing to cue! Not such a tough shoot".

Patty: "The hardest part may've been the make-up. It took a long time and it was quite heavy".

Kathy: "Leaving! We all got on well".

Mak: "There wasn't a hardest part. It was an easy day".

Julia: "Having lip gloss applied every 3 seconds!"

What was it like working with Robert Palmer?

Julie: "He was polite & the ultimate professional...and of course he was exceptional at performing on cue! We had very little interaction with him because...

1. He clinched the song in a few takes so the group filming was very fast.
2. He seemed rather intimidated by 5 ladies towering above him.
3. His wife was present...!

Clearly if Robert Palmer had been a heartthrob of my generation, I would've been less blasé about his presence!"

Patty: "Robert Palmer was always a professional & a gentleman. He took great care of us always".

Kathy: "It was great, he was very friendly and happy with the shoot".

Mak: "Well, he's a legend... & was a humble guy with it. You could tell he was a hard-working man who took his music seriously. I had a conversation with him about his using Sly and Robbie, a Jamaican drum & bass duo, on his L.P.. I asked him about what it was like to work with them".

Julia: "He was very polite if a little remote (his wife was there!)".

What did they think of the video?

Julie: "Loved it! I thought it was totally original and I loved the passion it evoked from many walks of life. It did and still does appeal across the generations".

Patty: "I think that the video is fantastic. It's an icon in the world of music videos!"

Kathy: "I thought it was great, very '80s".

Mak: At the time I was so embarrassed. I didn't really do that kind of overtly sexy modelling. I did more sophisticated stuff or fresh-faced smiley shoots. This was really vampy and the reactions I got from folk when they realized that I was one of the girls started to freak me out. I couldn't understand why that video was getting so much attention. Why we were considered so sexy...?"

Julia: "I hated it at the time, as it was me up there but now as I'm older I can be more objective & I think it's great".

What had their parents thought of it?

Julie: "Of it, or of me in it? Interestingly, I've never asked them but I sensed pride and relief that this gave an indication of good things to come".

Patty: "My parents couldn't believe it. They saw it way before I did but most likely didn't even know it was me. I never told them about anything that I was doing. They lived in America & we didn't have cell phones back then, so we didn't speak that frequently. When I spoke to them, I rarely spoke to them about work!"

Kathy: "I think they were just happy that I was getting work!"

Mak: They thought it was great, didn't have a problem with it at all, not that either of them saw it for a while, because they didn't watch music videos, so they only saw it once it had started to get loads of attention".

Julia: "Difficult to tell, as they weren't into that kind of music, but overall pretty proud".

What had their friends thought of it?

Julie: "Friends in the modelling world were very gracious about it. Friends outside the modelling world thought it very cool, but made sure I kept my feet firmly on the ground!"

Patty: "I have no idea. We didn't see it much in England".

Kathy: "I think they thought that it was quite cool to be a part of such a talked-about video".

Mak: "They were the ones who were telling me, 'Mak, you have no idea how massive the video is and how impressed or infatuated folk are with your appearance in it'. I was so busy travelling that I hadn't really cottoned on to how huge it had become. I'd get really shy (still do to an extent!) if they'd tell people in front of me that I was the 'bass player' because all of a sudden they get all 'No! Really? Wow!' or sometimes get a weird look on their faces, especially boys…ahem…".

Julia: My friends thought it was great, although I was overseas when it 1st came out, so some of the

impact was lost.

Had the video ever affected their dating lives in any way, as when they'd 1st told boyfriends they were in it?

Julie: "Ha…I can't imagine any of us bragging to our boyfriends about being in the video but one way or another they seemed to find out".

Patty: "I never really mentioned the video to anyone, mostly because I stayed in Europe until the early '90s. If anyone knew though, it always led to a fun conversation. Folk were pretty taken by how popular it was. In hindsight I feel like the video may've been more popular than the song itself".

Kathy: "I'd love to say yes, but I don't think so. I had an ex who was a drummer—he loved it!"

Mak: "Ummm…well, I was in a long-term relationship at the time, but since then it's not something I'd introduce myself as, but when I tell whoever, they tend to be quite impressed…"

Julia: "I've never been proactive in telling people (too English!), having let people know only when I knew them a little better, but when they've found out, they've been pretty amazed!"

Had they received fan mail? If so, did they still have any of it?

Julie: "Not that I remember. Google wasn't invented yet! so it wasn't easy to track us down. Maybe Julie Pankhurst, who founded UK social networking site 'Friends Reunited' has been inundated with 'Addicted to Love' fan mail!"

Patty: "I'm sure I did, but I didn't take it very seriously!"

Kathy: "No, definitely not…but the agency got a lot of calls…"

Mak: "I still receive fan mail, but via email or folk following me on Twitter @_ms_mak".

Julia: "I used to get some sent to my agent when I was modelling, but I haven't kept anything. Some guy on the Internet set up a fan page of me".

Julie had sent 2 versions of the sleeve/cover to the single; was that her on both of them?

Julie: "Yes".

Did she know why they'd chosen her, and had the others said anything about it?

Julie: "I haven't a clue why I got to grace the covers. I haven't really thought about it before but I'm sure the girls didn't lose any sleep over it. It was shot by a photographer named Ashworth & designed by Island Art. I'm assuming they're connected to Island Records".

Had the video generated any controversy that they knew of?

Julie: "It did. Ironically I imagine that's partly why it became such a cult video of the '80s".

Patty: "Not that I know of".

Kathy: "Not that I know of, although as it was copied so much, it can only be good…"

Mak: "I think there were discussions at the time at the objectification of women. I think that missed the point, though. The brief from Terence Donovan was to look like shop window mannequins. I guess his reasoning was that in so many videos women were being blatantly objectified, so why not poke fun at that and offer something they'll never be able to get hold of. We didn't have a come-hither look in our eyes. It was a look but you can't touch. We were dangerous ornaments. Out of reach & perfect accessories to Mr. Palmer's bespoke tailored suit".

Julia: "Yes, it had the feminists up-in-arms. They felt it was a bad portrayal of women. I always thought it was a great video, with very powerful images of women looking in control".

What were they paid?

Julie: "We were paid £500, which was the standard rate for pop videos back then, but bearing in mind the mega-bucks it generated…peanuts!"

Patty: "I think we were paid £250 / day. I don't really recall but I remember thinking that it was very little. Now that I look back, I know that it was very little!"

Kathy: "A few hundred pounds".

Mak: ";o)"

Julia: "I can't remember. I know it was good, as I was more excited with the fee than the fact that I had got the video!"

Had they watched the MTV World Premiere of the video, and if so, where & how did that feel?

Julie: "I didn't see it, but we quickly became aware that it was one of MTV's most popular videos at the time".

Patty: "No".

Kathy: "No, I missed it, as I was working in Japan at the time".

Mak: "No, didn't even know they had one. I was so busy working".

Julia: "I missed it! I was modelling in Japan at the time".

Were they ever recognized in public? If so then how often and when was the last time? Had they got any stories about it?

Julie:" It's funny that we've been recognized in public, considering that the slicked-back hair and pouty red lips isn't the usual morning make-up routine, but occasionally it has happened. Apparently they guess from the eyes. The school playground was one of the more recent times, prior to my son's knowledge of it, so I can't hold him responsible!. That spread like wildfire!"

Patty: "I was never recognized, I think that this was quite on purpose. Terence wanted all of the women to be unrecognizable…ambiguous, vague, obscure…that was the point. Beautiful, sexy women…but they could've been anyone".

Kathy: "No, sorry!"

Mak: "Never. The make-up and hair made me look completely different than how I do in real life".

Julia: "I have a lot of folk say that they recognize me from something but they can't put their finger on what. It's an easy video to go incognito".

Had they appeared in any other music videos after that?

Julie: "With Harry Connick, Jr. in 'Recipe for Love'. Patty & I were in the Robert Palmer 'Simply Irresistible' U.S. Pepsi commercial in 1989".

Patty: Yes, I did, again with Robert Palmer, in 'I Didn't Mean to Turn You On' then again in the Pepsi advert with Robert singing 'Simply Irresistible'.

Mak: "There was a Bryan Ferry one, but you can't really see me in it".

Had they ever met any other women who were female leads in a mainstream '80s rock video?

Julie: "Yes, but foggy memory cells = I've forgotten whom".

Patty: "I know that there are many, but I no longer know them".

Kathy: "No, I didn't".

Mak:"I can't think of any off the top of my head, but there must be models that I know who've done some".

Julia: "Debra Lang was with my agency and a friend. She was in a Queen video and ended up marrying Roger Taylor".

Had they gone to college, if so where & what had they studied?

Julie: "I trained in childcare then launched into modelling after a few years, as a nanny for a photographic agent and commercials director".

Patty: "I went to UCLA during the '90s to study art history. I did my internship at a photography gallery named G. Ray Hawkins, which specialized in the sale of vintage photographs. 15 years later, I went back to the extension program at UCLA to study horticulture".

Kathy: "No, I left school at 16, having been scouted by a model agent".

Mak: "The London College of Printing, Graphics & Design".

Julia: "I didn't go to university. I was modelling from the age of 16".

What had they been doing lately?

Julie: "Enjoying work and motherhood. Dabbling with the properties I bought thanks to a lucrative modelling career. I've been retailing Indian leather bound journals in the UK for some years - any excuse to indulge in the culture of that country - but this is now taking a back-seat to a business I started after having my son. It's an online mail order company selling an eclectic mix of children's gifts—anything from frothy tutus and sparkly shoes to educational science museum kits. Another excuse to travel far & wide to design and source new products".

Patty: "I work with landscape designers and architects. I have 2 children, having got married on June 22nd, 2013 in Los Angeles".

Kathy: "I'm living in Phuket, Thailand, being involved with various charities. I'm on the board of a charity set up by my late friend, Tom McNamara—the 'Phuket Has Been Good to Us Foundation', providing English classes to the underprivileged. I'm also on the board of 'The Good Shepherd Phuket', an organization that helps school the children of migrant Burmese workers and helps women who've been trafficked for the sex trade".

Mak: "A bit of modeling from time to time, but my main focus & energy is on the 'Edible Bus Stop' (@EdibleBusStop), a project I co-founded a couple of years ago. We've had some great publicity and last year were invited to 10 Downing Street by the Prime Minister & were nominated for an Observer Ethical Award, the Green Oscars".

Julia: "I'm a hair and make-up artist".

When had Kathy moved to Thailand & why?

Kathy: "About 12 years ago. I fell in love with the people and the country then my husband started working there".

Where did the others live?

Julie: "Still loving the buzz of London".

Patty: "Los Angeles".

Mak: "Brixton, London".

Julia: "London".

If ever married, what was their future husband's reaction when discovering that they were in the video?

Julie: "Quietly impressed and amused by the impact that it stirred up, but the video was part & parcel of a long modelling career, so in itself it didn't have much impact on our lives".

Patty: "My ex-husband, Jonathan Elias, wrote the original score for the MTV music show 'the MTV jingle'. It was a sweet part of our meeting".

Kathy: "I'm married now, but at the time we were friends and he thought it was great".

Mak:" ;o)"

Julia: "He was, I think, a little shocked & probably didn't entirely believe me!"

Interesting that the man behind the MTV theme wed the lead woman of one of the most iconic MTV videos. How had Patty met Jonathan—was it via the MTV connection?

Patty: "I met Jonathan at a birthday party through mutual friends. We didn't connect our MTV experiences until later, maybe on our 2nd or 3rd date. Jonathan is a composer who was living in New York in the '80s, working with Duran Duran at the time".

What did her current husband do?

Patty: "My new husband, Michael Rosenfeld, is a real estate developer in Los Angeles".

Any children?

Julie: "An 8-year-old boy".

Patty: "Lilli Elias, 17, and Jack Elias, 12".

Kathy: "No kids, but 9 godchildren who reacted over the years with 'Wow, that's great!' to 'How embarrassing!'"

Mak: "No".

Julia: "2 girls, 13 & 7 years old".

What did they think of the video?

Julie: "My son thinks it's very cool, having recently started telling anyone who'll listen that his mum was in a famous video. The low profile is now in jeopardy".

Patty: "They think it's hysterical. It's hard for them to believe that mommy had such a glamorous life!"

Julia: "They think it's 'cool' - their word!"

What had they thought when they were first asked for the interview?

Julie: "Is he legit?"

Patty: "Hmmmm".

Kathy: "Oh God, it was such a long time ago".

Mak: "'Gosh, that video will never leave me! LOL!"

Julia: "Another interview!"

What other interviews about the video had they given?

Julie: "I'm flaky about who/what/when. Ask Mak...".

Patty: "I've had offers to be interviewed a lot. I don't take it very seriously. I did a show back in '94...not sure what it was. Lame interview".

Kathy: "The 'News of the World' did a 'Where are they now?' article a while ago".

Mak: "Loads! I can't even begin to name them all!"

Julia: "We've given quite a few over the years; the 'I Want My MTV' book, and a show for VH1 titled 'Video Vixens'".

It had been difficult to find Patty. How had the others located her?

Patty: "Folk have tracked me down through my old agency in London,' Models 1', or through word of mouth. I never answer!".

When Patty said that she didn't take interview requests very seriously, did that mean she said no to most of them? If so, what made her agree to this one?

Patty: "Throughout the last 20 years, I've heard many folk reference the 'Addicted to Love' video & discuss who the girls are or were. It's always so funny to hear people talk as if they know! Most folk really have no clue who the original girls were…including me! I think it was me, Julie Pankhurst, Julia, Mak, and who? So you can see that I don't take this very seriously… but it was so nice to hear from Julie Pankhurst! How can anyone say no to Julie? I'd love to see her!"

Had they appeared at any fan conventions to sign autographs? If not, would they?

Julie: "I haven't done so. Never say never".

Patty: "No, I haven't. I'd do it just to see all of the girls!"

Kathy: "No & no".

Mak: "No".

Julia: "No, but maybe…"

Had they stayed in touch with Robert Palmer and/or each other after the shoot?

Julie: "Not with Robert Palmer but I worked many times with Donovan. We girls often saw each other through work - Mak & Patty were also with Models 1. Patty became a good friend when we both spent time in Australia at the end of the '80s. We lost touch when she moved back to the States but I'm hoping you can track her down so that we can get back in touch! Julia and I are great friends. I haven't seen Kathy for years. I became a photographic agent when I stopped modelling & last saw her at a fantastic exhibition she organized for 'Fashion Acts Aids' charity. Our photographers donated some photos to help raise money for it".

Patty: "I was lucky to stay in touch with Robert and his management team for a few years since we were still working together. Then, we all carried on…I moved back to America during 1991 then stopped modelling soon after".

Kathy: "No contact with Robert, but I stayed in touch with Julia".

Mak: "Not Mr. Palmer, but occasionally me & a couple of the girls get brought together for a shoot or interview".

Julia: "I saw Robert on a shoot a few years before he sadly died. I'm good friends with Julie and see her once a month".

When was the last time that they'd been in touch with each other?

Julie: "Mak, 2006—VH1 feature; Patty, early '90s; Kathy, mid-'90s—Fashion Acts exhibition; Julia, weekly".

Patty: "I really haven't been in touch with any of them. I always ask about Mak and Julie—both such loves!"

Kathy: "Not for a long time…until a week ago, April 2013, when Julia sent me a message about this interview".

Mak: "Last year".

Julia: "I'm Facebook friends with Mak & Kathy, but don't seem to have enough time to see them. Would love to though".

Mak, Julie and Julia re-enacted the video at Julia's wedding reception in 2013:
"Just an adoring line of women in front of us, whooping & cheering along,
and behind them stunned men, not quite knowing what to do with themselves".
Mak: "You can even credit me as happily divorced! Ha ha!"

How had they found out that Robert Palmer had died during 2003?

Julie: "In the news".

Patty: "I was sitting in my kitchen listening to the news. I was still so sad that Johnny Cash had just died a week or so before. It really isn't fair. Robert was way too young".

Kathy: "On the radio. It was incredibly sad".

Mak: "A friend texted me. Was very sad to hear it".

Julia: "From national television".

How did they look back on the experience?

Julie: "With a smile".

Patty: "The experience is & was just fantastic. It's such a funny little detail to have about oneself. Not everyone can say that they were lucky enough to participate in a piece of music history. I feel blessed!"

Kathy: "With pride to be part of video history".

Mak: "I had no idea at the time it was to become so iconic or such a pivotal moment in music videos. I was very successful at the time and it didn't register for me, as I was more focused on getting high-end magazine covers & big campaigns. With hindsight, of course, I acknowledge it. It's a legacy that I'm proud to be a part of".

Julia: "Now that I'm older I think it was an amazing thing to have been part of and I'm so glad I got to work with Terence Donovan & 4 of the coolest girls that I've ever met".

Was there anything that they'd like to add?

Julie: "A few years ago, a student from Australia asked for help with his college project about iconic women of the '80s. I don't have his questions but here are excerpts from my reply:

'I did this video at the beginning of my modelling career, which was a great introduction for other work. I got jobs directly as a result of the video but also because of working with Donovan. I was the keyboard player in the video. At the time of filming, nobody had any idea that it'd be so iconic. Robert Palmer had apparently issued the song previously without a video, but it had bombed, so they were taking a big financial risk by re-releasing it.

The director Terence Donovan came up with the concept for the video, his intention being to portray strong, confident women—hence the black dresses, slicked hair, and red lips—known at that time as 'power dressing', but there were two issues of protest. Firstly there was a feminist uproar. They felt that we were portrayed as sexual objects & as such, 'exploited'. We didn't feel we were doing womanhood an injustice!

From our perspective, the image of us Donovan had hoped to portray in the video was indicative of the assertiveness of women in the UK during the '80s. We had a very strong female Prime Minister, Margaret Thatcher, who was an inspiration for many women. 2ndly, the musicians union initially banned the video from mainstream television because we were models, not musicians, 'playing' instruments. From what I understood at the time, we weren't allowed to imitate playing instruments.

The late Terence Donovan had been a very successful photographer/director since the '60s. He tended to select models that were both good looking and confident, that criteria being applicable to this video. The song is about addictions. Due to the nature of the lyrics, we were directed to show little expression. Robert Palmer sang about obsessive emotions, so in contrast we reciprocated with little emotion.

Robert shot the video with us but was quite shy. He didn't want to be remembered for the 'Addicted to Love' girls. He had a successful career before the video, but this & his subsequent videos definitely revived his career, having attracted a whole new audience, although the videos tended to eclipse him, so he didn't appreciate the attention we were getting, which was rather ungracious considering that he made millions from the songs to these videos!

We were asked to do a show with Palmer in Spain but we all declined due to work commitments. We've done occasional TV appearances/press but on the whole we've not outwardly sought publicity. Tons of girls have claimed to be in the video, which generally doesn't bother us but we did complain to the UK press for publishing high-profile articles about Susie Verrico, a contestant on the UK Big Brother program, as they printed an image of me alongside her claim to be the keyboard player. The British press also stated that she was a stripper, so naturally we didn't want to be associated with her!"

Patty: "Good luck! Let's get all of the girls together. I've a feeling that you could do it!"

All 5 girls did indeed reunite for the 1st time since their 1986 shoot on 14th June 2014.

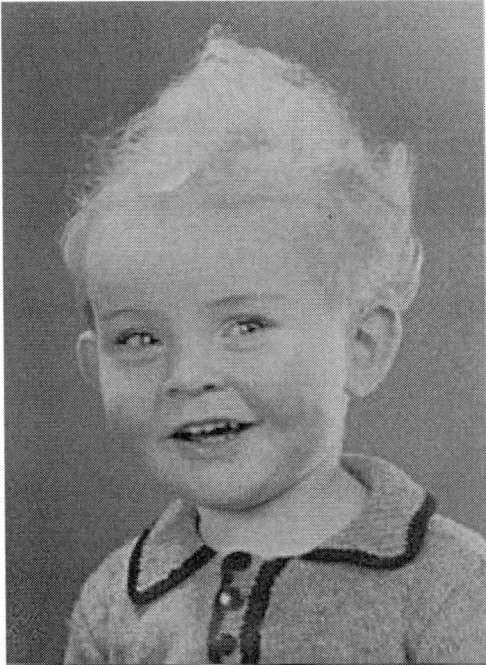

ROBERT PALMER · RIPTIDE

ROBERT
PALMER

ROBERT PALMER

Printed in Great Britain
by Amazon